FRIENDSHIP HOUSE

HOMELESS HOSPITALITY

Linda Pettit

CONTENTS

PREFACE

It was 1989, and I had just begun working for Skagit Mental Health and PORTAL as a liaison to help support clients wishing to move into the county. There was a need for housing affordable to those with limited incomes, as well as ongoing medical support. I began getting to know various people in the community, and was introduced to Barbara Cram. Friendship House had been operating for about three years then, and Barb was very interested in developing ongoing housing. I was contacted by Tim White, who was considering purchase of the property on South Second Street, to be remodeled into low income housing.

A dear family friend at the time was Clifford Burke, a local writer, printer and poet. He contacted me after acquiring a movie camera for the first time in his life. He was excited about getting to know how to use it and he shot footage of our family outdoors. He was interested in seeing the Friendship House, and talked with Barbara Cram, whom he knew. She took him on a tour of the house, which he filmed. Then he made a video copy of the film and gave it to us.

Early this year, 2015, I was looking at some of the videos we still have in a cabinet (ah, history!) and came across that film. I have maintained connection with Friendship House all these years as a supporting donor, and know the amazing development of this powerful community service site. I thought, "Wow! This is history to be shared!" And I began meeting with former board members whom I had known when I served on the Board. Through the months I met and interviewed Barbara Cram's partner, Pat Simpson, who gave me much historic info and pictures. I have interviewed all the other living Directors, as well as many other supportive figures.

Friendship House has grown into a strong local manifestation of the power of those who truly desire to be helpful to people who are without homes and support. Homeless hospitality is more than just providing a place to eat and sleep, although this is fundamental, of course. It is also about recognizing the truth of individual being, giving longer term support for those who are ready to truly change their lives, and accepting visitors with love. There will be a celebration for the 30th Anniversary of Friendship House in 2016, on May 26. I am hoping to have this history available for this event!

Linda Pettit

INTRODUCTION

The United States has experienced people who needed help to survive poverty and lack of resources since the founding of the nation.

"Poverty was viewed as a temporary condition, a result of hard times. Poor relief was straightforward. Those in need received assistance at home--food, fuel, and money--paid for out of the poor tax levied separately from other taxes on every Boston household. The few homeless, and those too desperate to sustain themselves at home, stayed at the almshouse."[1]

By the 1820's, Almshouses had developed into a model that included work within to help provide for their support. This development was influenced by English practices, with the thought of correcting the laziness of their inmates. By the end of the 19th century, Edgar J Helms, a minister called to work with inner-city missions, had developed the concept of community church for the poor, with training in various industries, music and crafts. Eventually this powerfully successful system developed into Goodwill Industries.

The United States moved into the Great Depression following the stock market crash in October 1929. This led to a steep decline in industrial output and serious unemployment. A million farms were lost and there were two million homeless people. The drought in the Middle Western Dust Bowl sent thousands of people to seek shelter where they could find it.

Individuals and families continued to find challenges throughout the nation, as employment prospects developed and changed. Beginning in 1930 with the Great Depression, these problems became powerfully and universally present. Locally cobbled together housing termed "Hoovervilles" developed by the hundreds in the USA. There were dozens in Washington. Seattle's main Hooverville was one of the largest, longest-lasting and best documented in the nation. Covering nine acres with a population up to 1200, it claimed its own community government including an unofficial mayor. It was on Port of Seattle property; police burned it twice but residents rebuilt it. Eventually a new mayor supported it and it survived for ten years, until the start of WWII.

After the war ended, the US began a period of prosperity with growing numbers of jobs in industries of many sorts. Some people remained at

---

[1]   Kathleen Hirsch "*Songs from the Alley*" 1989

the bottom, but the majority did well for decades. Washington State grew in population and the Puget Sound seemed like a very good place to live, drawing people from all over the world. Seattle experienced a shock with the "Boeing Bust" in 1970, but the airline industry persisted and employment was well sustained. Homelessness was not apparent to the average citizen.

Skagit County, Washington in the early 1980's had a growing awareness of the need for housing homeless people. Located next to the I-5 freeway, Mount Vernon found numbers of passersby pulling off the highway, as well as people who participated in the PORTAL program (Program Offering Residential Training in Adult Living) for mental health treatment on the former site of Northern State Hospital in Sedro Woolley. There were support services available for the discharged patients, but some would relapse and be drawn into difficult relationships.

An informal group of concerned citizens from several different churches began to discuss issues in Mount Vernon, referring to themselves as the Peace and Justice Committee. These included Father Michael Holland, a Catholic priest; the priest from the Episcopal Church; ministers from the Lutheran and Presbyterian churches; and concerned church members.

By 1983 there was an Emergency Shelter Committee. The Sedro Woolley Saint Vincent de Paul Church and the Salvation Army joined to sponsor rental of a motel room, to be increased with need. A volunteer coordinator was appointed. This agreement was good through the end of September 1983, then was furthered by petitions. Skagit County Community Action Agency then coordinated. Funding was gained for partial need through September 1984. A proposal was designed for fundraising and operations.

By July 1985, the motel facilities were withdrawn. Need was being unmet due partly to limitations from the DSHS Consolidated Emergency Program. Requests were increasing; no one could get more than five days service totally. There were no shelters in Skagit Valley. In August 1985, Neighbors in Need proposed using a block grant to allow the former Bethany Covenant Church on Evergreen Street to provide emergency housing. While the Mount Vernon City Planner received a letter from a representative at DSHS supporting this grant request, emergency housing did not manifest quickly and remained an ongoing problem.

GENESIS OF HOPE FOR THE HOMELESS

By early 1986, a core group of supporters that included the "Three Barbaras"; Barbara Evans Cram, Barbara Evans (now Schaeffer), and Barbara "Buzzy" Marsh - along with Sharon Bell - identified the need for a permanent homeless shelter in Skagit Valley. Local groups of supporters (later known as The Peace and Justice Committee) had met for a couple of years with discussion about how and where this shelter could happen. The Skagit Valley Hospitality House Association was incorporated as a 501(c)(3) non-profit on March 12, 1986. Friendship was always a key principle in the discussions and the shelter would become known as Friendship House informally.

Mission Statement

We must first accept ourselves. Not as we would like to be, but as we are.

As we share from our surplus, we respond to the poor; from our poverty, recognizing that to do so supplies our own needs.

Hospitality -- There are no strangers here, only friends we haven't met.

We feel the need to network with other resources in order to be an advocate for those who come to us.

The group found an older single-family house, converted to four apartments on South Third Street. It was located across the street from the then Salem Lutheran Church and was owned by Barbara Evan's husband Ken who offered the property to the organization with $10 down.

"I don't think they ever cashed the check," said Cram, "Friendship House supporters started work with a crowbar..."

After dinner in the first year. Buzzy Marsh plays for the sing-along.

Barb Cram welcomes a newcomer.

The house had to become shared space for 25 people; men, women, and children, and had to be extensively renovated by volunteers.

Original funding of $700 came from the Presbyterian Church's Synod of Alaska-Northwest, and $6000 raised from the first local board members. Friendship House opened in September 1986 as "truly a grassroots community effort," Cram remembered.

They opened the doors on blind faith and were quickly overwhelmed. The House was crowded with 25 initial guests; by 1989 the monthly average was 40, sleeping on 23 beds and six couches.

"After that it's mats on the floor," said Cram, when they ran out of floor space.

New kitchen addition on the first house.

FOUNDATIONAL CONCEPTS

During the Great Depression one of the activists who responded to the difficult conditions involving homelessness was a journalist working for social causes named Dorothy Day. She co-founded "The Catholic Worker" newspaper in 1933 which had an initial press run of 2500; within two years the circulation had grown to 150,000. Eventually The Catholic Worker occupied its own building in New York City. There was always coffee and a pot of soup on the stove, and anyone coming to the door was welcome to share a meal. Word got around, and by 1936, a crowd of hundreds was lining up at the door each day.

Gradually, other houses began to spring up across the country--more than thirty of them in the first ten years--and The Catholic Worker was truly a movement. Though affiliated with the headquarters in New York and following the principles espoused in the paper, each house was quite independent, adapting its style and organization to its own circumstances and needs. Nevertheless, a surprising degree of consistency existed (as it does still) among different Worker communities, characterized by a spirit of functional anarchy, an abhorrence of regulations, and a basic tolerance for persons of all backgrounds. In contrast to many intentional communities, with members carefully screened for personal and ideological compatibility, the Worker community consisted of whoever showed up at the door. The result was often an assemblage of characters seemingly drawn from a novel by Dostoevsky. On hand in most Catholic Worker houses was a similar cast of pilgrims, scholars, and "holy fools," the young and old, workers, loafers, and everything in between. It was a microcosm of sorts, a family, as Dorothy would say, and an example of the possibility of a diverse group of individuals residing together in a relative harmony, without the need for elaborate rules. The basis for community was not an ideal to be achieved, but the recognition of a reality already accomplished in Christ--the fact that all, whether clever or dull, fit or infirm, beautiful or plain, were "members one of another."[2]

The Art and Practice of Hospitality

"Do not neglect to show hospitality, for by that means, some have entertained angels without knowing it." Hebrews 13.2

Hospitality is essentially an attitude which influences how we go about

---

2   Robert Ellsberg "Title" 1983

being with others in a simple, human, and healing way. This stance of hospitality is the heart and soul of any service offered to people.

Hospitality is an ancient concept which has been a significant value in every civilization, culture, and religion. The expression of hospitality throughout the ages was essentially that of unquestioning openness to the stranger, who was considered a friend. The concept of hospitality has lost much of its meaning and influence in our contemporary society, where alienation is a common condition. Renewing the practice of this ancient art humanizes the community in a world full of strangers.

Henri Nouwen[3] defines hospitality as "the creation of a free space where the stranger can enter and become a friend instead of an enemy. Hospitality is not to change people, but to offer them space where change can take place. We cannot...change other people by our convictions, stories, advice, and proposals, but we can offer a space where people are encouraged to disarm themselves, to lay aside their occupations and preoccupations and to listen with attention and care to the voices speaking in their own center."

Hospitality is a gift *shared* by equals. There is no room for condescension or the "giver's complex" in the genuine practice of hospitality. The hospitable stance is an acknowledgment of our solidarity with one another in the joys and pains of life. Hospitality cannot be given away, but only shared.

We cannot make out of hospitality a business, or allow it to go the way of many human services in our society which are rendered in a heartless, judgmental manner bearing absolutely no signs of human compassion. Nouwen speaks to this danger in the phrase "cure without care."

"In a community like ours we have put all the emphasis on cure. We want to be professionals: heal the sick, help the poor, teach the ignorant, and organize the scattered. But the temptation is that we use our expertise to keep a safe distance from that which really matters, and forget that in the long run cure without care is more harmful than helpful."[4]

Three Dimensions of Hospitality

Hospitality is a response. It responds to those who have entered our free and open space; it responds to the human conditions which are revealed because of our openness.

---

3   Henri Nouwen "*Reaching Out*" 1975

4   Henri Nouwen "Out of Solitude" 1974

There are three dimensions of hospitality: service, advocacy, and community awareness. Each dimension is not only a type of response, but is essential to the genuine practice of hospitality.

1. *Service* is the response to human need as it presents itself through people who enter our lives. It is the first and most natural response. It is the major focus of Friendship House.

2. *Advocacy* is responding to the causes of the human needs. Once a person's needs have been met through service, genuine hospitality is compelled to respond to the factors which created that need. Once we offer service, we cannot be satisfied that this is sufficient. Through advocacy, we share in people's struggle for a whole life by seeking positive changes.

3. *Community Awareness* is that dimension of hospitality which presents to the broader community what we know of the suffering of its members. We can speak of this dimension as community awareness or community education, but what it will ultimately accomplish is community change.

The art of hospitality is complete when practiced to the full extent of these three dimensions.

COMMUNITY REACTION

Local Politics

The Mount Vernon City Council was initially very encouraging of the development of services for the homeless population as recorded in Council Meeting Minutes.

In August 1989, Mayor Reep, along with Council members Bordner and Cheney, had dinner at the original Friendship House.

"A lot of people are giving a lot of time and money toward this worthwhile project." Mayor Reep stated in City Council Minutes[5].

Women's House

Barbara Cram and Buzzy Marsh addressed the Council in 1989, requesting $20,000 to buy and upgrade a second house to serve women and children. The requested amount was a down payment, not the purchase price.[6]

Mayor Reep presented Barbara Evans Cram with a plaque for Mayor's Citizen of the Year Award for 1989. He stated that, at the last meeting, he had presented a similar plaque to Buzzy Marsh and that he appreciated all of their hard work. Ms. Cram stated that they appreciated the cooperation of the City and the citizens of Mount Vernon.

"A project such as Friendship House doesn't just happen, but is the result of a lot of hard work by a lot of people."[7]

Backyard play area, 2014.

In October 1991, Teddie Chapman of the Friendship House Board addressed the Council, requesting the title

---

5   Mount Vernon City Council Minutes 8/9/1989
6   Mount Vernon City Council Minutes 11/21/1989
7   Mount Vernon City Council Minutes 2/14/1990

transfer for the second Friendship House to qualify for $6000 in 1991 City funds.[8] In June 10, 1992, a donation of was finally authorized.[9]

Neighborhood Resistance

Not everyone in the community was supportive of having homeless shelters in the middle of town.

After Friendship House had been in operation for several years, there was a growing awareness of the numbers of homeless that needed help, and continued to arrive at the shelter daily. Unknown people moving through the streets in the neighborhood where businesses had offices was very disturbing to some in the community.

By 1993, the Mount Vernon City Council had started to receive letters from Friendship House neighbors complaining about various issues involving homeless people in the area.

Some businesses nearby the houses felt that servicing the population was disturbing to the more professional offices and a rezone was requested. In response, the City assembled numerous regulations they would like to see governing shelters, including types, occupancy, length of stay, hours of operation, staffing, location and parking requirements. In addition they recommended that a shelter be at least one thousand feet from any other group home or shelter care facility, that it be licensed by an appropriate agency of the state, provide adequate off-street parking, and have an appearance conforming to the neighborhood.

A public hearing for the Homeless Shelter standards and Recommen- dations before the Planning Commission was held in October. The Planning Commission Adopted the City Planner's recommendations for shelters. The regulations were passed to the City Attorney, who created a new ordinance.[10]

In December 1993, the annual City contribution to Friendship House was reduced from $6000 to $3000. (This amount has varied over the years due to specific requests.)

The Council approved a request for the 1994 donation of $3000 to be used for renovating a bathroom in the women's house. This amount remained the annual support for several years. Various other amounts were requested by different directors, but the average $3000 is current today.

---

8   Mount Vernon City Council Minutes 10/9/1991
9   Mount Vernon City Council Minutes 6/10/1992
10   Chapter 17.48 C-2 GENERAL COMMERCIAL DISTRICT - 17.48.020.E

LEARNING FROM EXPERIENCE

Over the years, Friendship staff, board and supporters worked hard to address many issues. Despite some objections, the fundamental need for housing a population with difficult complexities was a great teaching. A roof is important, but support for deeper needs is essential.

Transitional Housing as done at Friendship House 1990-2002
By Buzzy Marsh, Friendship House Director, 1994-1998

Buzzy Marsh, Director

"When Friendship House came into existence we were all a little too naive when we set out to help the poor, especially the poor and homeless. Somehow we thought that giving homeless people a roof over their heads was the answer to a large part of their problems. That was only a very beginning piece of what we now know to be a very complicated problem and process of healing and re-education. It did, though, bring us into direct contact with the people we were trying to help. We soon learned that all people did not universally hold our middle class experiences and values; that our good and pleasant backgrounds weren't necessarily helpful when deciding what was needed. We needed to change and to think differently. We knew very little about life when it was reduced to basic survival. Survival against very difficult life experiences develops a view of life and a value system honed to help homeless people exist in crisis situations. Substandard early childhood care and difficult family situations were almost always a part of their less than ideal upbringing. A survival mode existence develops a whole lot of survival skills that do not always trust the system, parents or people trying to be helpful. Very often, survival skills lead to learning very quickly to con the system, to place their own needs as a priority. We as 'do-gooders' had to earn respect by our willingness to change our understanding of what were the 'real' problems of homelessness. We had to learn to listen. We had to provide safe housing, often safety from themselves and other homeless dangers, both situations and people. In a nutshell, it was a lot bigger problem than we first thought it to be. We had to admit that we couldn't handle all these presenting problems, let alone know the solutions. But, we were determined to get to work trying.

"Our first attempt to provide transitional housing began because of two factors. One was the problem of trying to help homeless single fathers. It is very hard to provide the proper space for little ones in a shelter where two or more people, sometimes up to six people, share bedrooms. While we could provide good meals and much company, there was often too much company and we weren't always sure about the safety of that company. The second necessary factor was to have access to a house within our financial capability. Puget Power owned a rental house located a couple of blocks away from Friendship House and they were willing to let us use the house just for the cost of the insurance ($100). Our part of the deal was to maintain the building and supervise the occupants. So began the history of the development of our Transitional Housing Program."

This arrangement started in 1990 and lasted about a year, but did not work well because there were no set rules in place. Rules began based on those used at Friendship House regarding drinking, drugging and cleanliness, as well as regular meetings with staff to problem solve. With very little money for housing, connection with other social agencies and homeowners began. There were several project sites for the next few years, including Skagit Mental Health. The housing that did not have ongoing individual counseling support worked for a few years, but eventually failed due to problems with addictions, overnight guests who stayed long term, and incompatible personalities.

It was observed that unless a person had lived in one of the Friendship houses, they had not experienced community living in a way that would prepare them to understand living as a community in the transitional house setting. The house managers observed and recommended those willing to cooperate with others, work together, and observe rules. These guests then became candidates for the workshop.

A major success was the opening of Oak House in Burlington in 1997. This is a large five-bedroom house with an area suitable for a parent and child. More time was taken in the workshop and planning stage. A set of basic rules and expectations were defined:

> No drinking.
> No drugs.
> No violence either verbal or physical.
> No overnight guests, other than visiting children.
> No smoking in the house.

The group within the house would make all decisions about daily management at community meetings held weekly. A Friendship House representative would be the moderator of these meetings. All policies and house decisions would be made by vote of members. Members were then committed to live by their own vote. These house policies could always be amended but only by the vote of the whole house community. Oak House was successful enough that the Friendship House Board decided to purchase the property.

At present, Transitional Housing is a functional part of the Friendship House community. There are currently two houses, Oak House in Burlington and another in Mount Vernon. Most of the residents are "alumni volunteers" who give back by cooking in the Cafe once a week or working in the pea patch garden. The program provides additional, longer-term support for people emerging out of homelessness and journeying into self-sufficiency. During their residency, he or she can work and save money to move into permanent housing. People can live in transitional housing for up to two years. They must first stay in the men's or women's shelter for two to three months so that they become known and their attributes assessed.

As is the case with Friendship House shelters and kitchen, the Transitional Housing program is the recipient of community generosity. Several years ago, an anonymous donor gave $20,000 towards the Oak House mortgage. In April 2012, the Jack and Shirley McIntyre Foundation paid off the entire mortgage in the amount of $80,276. Such generosity helps Friendship House keep its solid financial footing, which will benefit our neighbors in need for many years to come.

Cooperative Housing

Mental Health Services

In 1990, a joint committee formed by Friendship House, Skagit Mental Health, and PORTAL opened the South Second Street Cooperative. A program operating at the former Northern State Hospital in Sedro Woolley, PORTAL (Program Offering Residential Treatment in Adult Living) was a state facility that drew residents statewide for stabilization and work training. These members could stay up to two years, earning small stipends from their work practices which would be held in a private account available on discharge to help pay for housing. The Cottage Program operated in two houses (former doctor's homes) where they received training in shared living. After discharge, a number of patients chose to stay in Skagit County. Skagit Mental Health worked to help find suitable housing in the community.

Barbara Cram had begun working with Skagit Mental Health (SMH) to find support for Friendship House residents. Communication began with Linda Pettit, liaison between SMH and the PORTAL Cottage Program. A local businessman, Tim White, had become interested in developing a foreclosed property that had been a motel on South Second Street in Mount Vernon. He contacted Pettit and suggested that the property could be restored and made into housing for the disabled.

"I want to give back to the community," White stated.

The community residents lived independently in eight units, around a central building that held a common meeting space, kitchen and dining area. The front part of the building was made into a laundromat that the residents operated to help pay for utilities. Shared meals were prepared five days a week, with rotating cooking and dishwashing chores. Members governed themselves, setting and enforcing their own rules. Weekly meetings were held with help from Pettit, Marsh and Cram.

"Group members try to work out problems as they come up. They can be confrontive, but they can be confrontive in a plain way," said Cram.

The residents decided together who would be allowed to move into the apartments. Applicants had to attend two meetings before being voted on; when a resident moved in, they had a 30-day grace period in which members and the new occupant decided whether the arrangement was working.

Given the successful operation of South Second Street Community, White bought another piece of property to upgrade for a second cooperative community. This was located about half a block away from the Friendship House sites, and consisted of a large old Victorian era home, with three smaller buildings in back. It was named Snoqualmie House, after the street on which it was located. In 1991, the site was occupied by 11 residents. The operation of the new community was based on the model established at South Second Street, with referrals made from Skagit Mental Health and Friendship House. However, there was no associated business to operate.

The cooperative communities persisted for 11 years, during which White never raises the rent. However, the properties were sold in 2002, and the new owners promptly raised all the rents, forcing closure of the communities. Interestingly, the Snoqualmie House property eventually was purchased by Friendship House for the construction of Friendship House Cafe!

CAPITAL CAMPAIGN

In 1992 the Board launched a successful three-year Capital Campaign. Through individual three-year pledges, the campaign was able to:

Pay off four mortgages of over $125,000 on the two hospitality houses.

Pay for needed upgrades to both the women's and men's houses, especially the bathrooms.

Complete a much needed commercial kitchen upgrade at the men's house to service the men, women and children, and walk-in public with meals.

The campaign was undertaken to free up much needed monthly donations to be used for the care and feeding of the homeless residents, rather than paying almost $2000 per month to service the loans. The campaign was chaired by Teddie Chapman, with co-chairs Judy Menish and Ginny Body. The Board agreed to hire a Capital Campaign consultant, Dick Rose, to train them about running a successful venture, (i.e., the need to "spend money to make money".)

What followed was a fourteen-week awareness campaign to educate the community about homelessness. The campaign included educational forums, prayer vigils, newsletters and personal home visits, and culminated in a Community Campaign Celebration Banquet in January, 1992. The celebration kicked off the three-year financial pledge commitment period.

By fall 1992, the campaign had paid off a $27,000 mortgage on the Women's House and a $7000 mortgage on the Men's House. Paying off the first loan allowed the City of Mount Vernon to release previously designated funds for fire safety.

The second year of the campaign brought a new series of forums, including designating Friendship House as a beneficiary in planned giving. By November 1993, the final payment on the Men's House was made. The ongoing need for upgrade in the more than 80-year-old houses was addressed in the formation of a dedicated maintenance reserve in the goals of the campaign. At the end of 1994, the goal was achieved, paying off all mortgages on the women's house.

Hunger to Hope – The Friendship House Cafe

A major factor in people finding housing is employment. The job must pay well enough to maintain housing and cover living expenses. It is practically impossible for homeless people without jobs to achieve a home with no major aid. Even the 44% of homeless people who do have jobs still cannot break out of their homeless state.

We have learned a great deal from programs started in the 1980s to combat homelessness, including the number of resources that must be provided as people climb

Friendship House Cafe kitchen and seating.

out of homelessness. First, job training is a crucial piece. Second, people must have a place to live while in training. Third, once they complete their training and begin working, continued housing support (e.g. transitional housing) is required for some until they can achieve a stable salary and operating level.

In July 2012, Friendship House became the owner of 108 Snoqualmie Street, a large property near the main office. The land was developed into the Friendship House Cafe, a cafeteria that feeds the hungry and offers an education and employment program that trains homeless men and women in basic cooking skills.

Hunger to Hope provides a 12-week kitchen apprenticeship certificate program at no cost to participants. Program training includes: Quantity cooking methods, Preparing soups and salads, Nutrition & menu development, Kitchen management skills, Preparing Vegetables and fruits, Making side dishes, Preparing sauces and stocks, Cooking meats, Food safety and sanitation, and Kitchen measurements. Participation is limited to six apprentices, who need not be residents or guests of Friendship House.

Friendship House Cafe garden.

WHAT LIES AHEAD

When Friendship House opened in 1986, it was the only site for homeless services in Skagit County. Through the years there have been many struggles as well as community support, and today things are quite different.

Skagit County now partners with the National Alliance to End Homelessness. Skagit County Community Action Agency (SCCAA) supports the program for Homeless Emergency Rapid Housing, which meets initially with those needing housing, a part of the Federal Hearth Act. Data is gathered to help define the local needs, and a coordinated entry system funnels referrals to Friendship House and other county centers such as the SCCAA Family Shelter. Such referrals must prioritize the most needy.

Another local community source of support is Family Promise of Skagit Valley; a non-profit organization focused on helping homeless children and their families. Supported by a coalition of local churches, Family Promise feeds and houses homeless families overnight at host congregations. During the day guests are at work or at their day center, where staff give counseling services and assistance in job placement.

Director Tina Tate states:

"As the largest shelter provider in Skagit County, we believe it is our responsibility to you, our donors, and the community at large to continue to expand our services to help the ever growing homeless population. Skagit needs a very basic mental health shelter that will enlarge capacity for a day center where needy people can get off the street. And we will look to provide permanent rentals for stabilized folks who have been through our system."

If Friendship House can create a credible model of this notion of hospitality, then it may be offering other segments of our society a model which can be applied to the many other areas of human suffering in our contemporary world. The impact of hospitality in its truest, most simple human form can have an impact far beyond the measurements of any social science or governmental research teams. The value of hospitality genuinely lived out needs no statement of need or proof of success. It is a universal value and the responsibility of each person's suffering and joy; hospitality fulfills the basic truth of our solidarity with one another.

PERSONAL STORIES

Directors

To date, Friendship House has had six directors, all women. Although all came from different places and had different experiences, all were called to be helpful in addressing homelessness. Each was intensely involved with funding and development, communicating with events inside and outside the shelter. Following are their personal stories.

Barbara Evans Cram (1986-1993)

Barbara was born in Seattle in 1935. She grew up in a large extended family, and began helping care for her siblings and cousins at a young age. She was close to her grandmother, but family dynamics caused her to choose to move out on her own about age 13. She went to two different high schools that challenged her bright, creative mind.

"I spent most of my high school years in despair," she recalled.

She took art classes at what was to become Seattle Community College.

"I thought I would grow up to be an artist," she recalled in an interview.

After graduating from Franklin High School in 1952, Cram enrolled in Central Washington University.

"I didn't fit in. I didn't like Eastern Washington. I was a city girl," she recalled.

She made a meager living in Seattle's University District for a while, drawing lightning-quick portraits and "playing beatnik." This lifestyle was short lived. A stint at Boeing was followed by ten years as a buyer for upscale I Magnin and Nordstrom's stores.

"I was working myself half to death, selling useless things to useless people. Life had to have more meaning," she recalled thinking.

During this period she married Dick Cram and had her son, Eric. They were divorced and later her daughter Marilynn was born. She also raised her niece Debbie, a girl with disabilities.

As a single mother of three, Cram enrolled in Western Washington University and discovered social work. She was selected to participate in New Careers for Washington, a "Great Society" program supported by Governor Dan Evans. "We were a ragtag bunch of welfare mothers and minorities. We worked half time and went to school half time," she said.

Her first assignment was at Northern State Hospital in Sedro Woolley in 1969, helping mental health patients find jobs and homes in the community. The hospital was working towards closing in a few years, although that was not clearly known at the time.

"I immediately fell afoul of the system," she recalled ruefully.

When a female patient complained of abuse in the house where she had been placed, Cram rebelled and brushed against politics and stiff-necked bureaucracy.

"I was an urban guerrilla, caught between the struggles of two departments," she mused.

Determined not to send vulnerable people into tough sections of Seattle, Cram established safe houses to ease transitions to living alone. Four group homes were established in West Seattle under the name of CONBELA (What the mind can CONceive and BElieve, the mind can Achieve). These were in safe neighborhoods, near recreational facilities, bus services and churches.

"They learned to live in the community by doing so," she noted.

The residents needed jobs, so Cram unleashed her business experience and established a sheltered workshop also called Conbela. The 47 workers produced hand silk-screened shirts and note cards.

Cram operated Conbela for five years before moving to Susanville, California. The town was centered unattractively near the Sierra Army Depot, a nuclear arms cache, and a state prison. After arriving and getting to know the community, she began to become aware of serious issues involving families of men who were inmates in the prison. Several wives with small children moved into the city in order to visit their husbands, but found that the prison was nine miles from the bus stop. They were faced with choosing a high taxi fare or walking with hopes of a ride. Cram searched out and assembled concerned people to form a chapter of "Friends Outside," which recognized that retention of strong family ties was the one prime force in the rehabilitation of released prisoners.

Under her, the group dug up funding for rental of a building to serve as a hospitality house, purchase a van for transportation of families from town to the prison, and to fund two positions.

This activity attracted requests for help from other ignored or hidden needs in the community-- a significant number of cases of family abuse and also an occurrence of quite a few local families without adequate food. Barbara Cram took on the task and provided a great amount of leadership and organization to form "Lassen Family Services" to assist abused family members and sponsor a crisis line, including getting required training for phone volunteers through Lassen Community College. The Susanville Community Food Shelf was formed to collect and dispense staple foods to people in need. After these services were organized, other volunteers took over the functions.

Cram worked as an instructor at Lassen Community College. She taught American History and Political Science, taught learning disabled adults, and acted as Dorm Facilitator to set up self-government for the residents, who were primarily Micronesian and inner-city disadvantaged youth.

After nine years in Susanville, Cram had to take time out to fight uterine cancer, a setback that was responsible for her eventual demise. In 1983 she returned to Skagit County, where she had spent part of the early 1960's running the Hope Island Resort for a friend. Her commitment to humanitarianism had grown even deeper after introduction to the Catholic Worker Movement.

"It's a way of doing things, a faith commitment to do what you can to improve the world," Cram said.

Addressing the identified local needs concerning homelessness, Cram readily became involved in the creation of Friendship House. She moved into the house when it opened in 1986, living there in her office for the first year of operation. Life quickly became intensely involved in addressing ongoing service needs, fundraising and coordinating with other local agencies. A Board of Directors was needed for the non-profit community, and dealing with the daily flow of potential residents required developing voluntary positions for assistance.

Barbara Cram and Friendship House began to draw attention from the county. She was presented with Mount Vernon Mayor's Citizen of the Year Award in 1989. By that year, the need for a second house to support women and children was apparent, and a house a couple of doors to the north was identified as desirable. Fundraising request for help to buy and upgrade the second house was presented to the Mount Vernon City

Council by Cram and Buzzy Marsh.

Board meetings were initially rather casual, often held in the shelter living rooms. As time passed, and board members became more professionally familiar with management proceedings, concerns began to develop about various issues. Cram was known for her resistance to seeking financial support that was not local and/or informal. She did not like keeping detailed records on paper.

The Catholic Worker Movement principles were aligned with this perspective. However, by 1992, Friendship House was holding four mortgages on the two houses, as well as having other maintenance issues. A Capital Campaign was identified by Board members as the process to address these concerns.

As the Capital Campaign developed through 1993, concerns about Barbara's lack of conventional management practices became a focus. It was determined that a different Director would be needed. Cram was a staunch character who was very capable of dealing with many historic issues. Her years of experience demonstrated what has been termed "Founder's Syndrome". At the end of the year, Barbara was officially retired and an evening of appreciation and celebration was held in her honor. As a token memorial the Men's House was renamed "The Barbara Evans Cram House."

Following her retirement, Barbara agreed to serve on the Board for three years. However, her "retirement" was a very painful personal experience, and she spent a year working on personal recovery of her feelings before moving to Seattle. Living with her dear friend Pat Simpson, Barbara became involved in local homeless housing projects for women and children, including Mary's Place which has developed and expanded greatly at this time.

After a large, happy 70th birthday celebration, Barbara developed lung cancer and eventually passed away in November 2009.

Barbara "Buzzy" Marsh (1994-1998)

Buzzy Marsh was born and raised in Yakima, in Eastern Washington. Raised in a Catholic family, when she graduated from high school she went to college at Seattle University, a Jesuit Catholic institution. In 1955, after acquiring a degree in Education, she became a second grade teacher at High Point Elementary School in West Seattle. The school was located in a neighborhood which historically included a low income population.

"I saw terrible needs there--few were being met," said Marsh.

Teaching was a most engaging experience, however, as she met many interesting people.

"At the school, the nurses and cooks helped care for the kids, making sure they had lunch. I rode from Seattle to West Seattle with teachers who were Japanese young people. The best teacher was a black woman who was in a wheelchair due to polio--it blew my prejudices!"

Buzzy taught for a year, then got married and became a mother of six children. After many years raising them, she and her husband were divorced, and she returned to Seattle University in 1982 to complete her MA degree in Theology, Pastoral Ministry and Family Counseling.

"I learned about negotiating, worked part time in an office supply store, and graduated in 1985."

Marsh came to Skagit County to start a five-parish youth ministry in the Catholic Church and her path crossed Barbara Cram's. She became connected with the Peace and Justice Committee involving local ministries concerned with homelessness in the county. As Friendship House continued to develop, she became a Board member. Finally the Board decided to take a faith venture and created the second paid position due to rapidly expanding workload and projects. Monthly income was variable and uncertain, but the position was created with the belief that the need would be addressed. Buzzy was then hired as co-director.

As Barbara Cram was retired at the end of 1993, Buzzy became interim Director; A search was made for a permanent Director and a candidate was identified and hired, but he did not show up for the job... So this temporary position became permanent in 1994.

Given the issues involved with the former director, Marsh set about developing managerial elements which were sorely needed. These included entry forms holding information about residents, and for the first time, a spread sheet with budgetary figures including costs per night. These basic fundamentals eventually enabled the acquisition of a computerized system to track guests with individual plans.

Buzzy Marsh was particularly concerned about the need for transitional housing that would help move Friendship House residents into safe places in the community. Here is her description from the *Introduction to Transitional Housing As Done at Friendship House (1990-2002)*.

"One of the first things we learned was that there was not enough housing. Not enough housing for the under-employed, not enough housing for the mentally ill, not enough housing that was clean and decent and affordable. Not enough housing that was in a safe area for single families, not enough ways that people could live together and survive. All of these problems became the milieu of our struggle to figure out the next best step for the guests who were ready to move out of Friendship House and continue to hold onto the growth and progress they had accomplished while in the shelter. These motives were the birth pangs of our efforts. We began to form a program of transitional housing just for the people that we knew and we were helping."

Working in partnerships with various agencies and property owners in the community resulted in a range of housing discussed in the Housing Section.

When Buzzy became 67 years old, she decided to retire from the position of Director eventually. She recommended that the Board hire Barbara Schaeffer, one of the founding planners, as the next Director, and this came to pass.

Buzzy Marsh remains involved with the Board and other activities of Friendship House, continuing communications through this day.

Barbara (Evans) Schaeffer (1999 – 2000)

Barbara Schaeffer grew up in Metaline Falls, a small town in Eastern Washington near the Canadian border. After graduating from high school in 1963, she went to Washington State University and earned a BA in Sociology. With this degree in hand she went to San Francisco and took a

job in the Mission District as a social worker, working with disabled people.

"It was weird, but I learned a lot."

Returning to Washington, Schaeffer studied at the University of Washington and completed work for a MA in Education. There she met and married Ken Evans, who would become an attorney. Together they moved to Mount Vernon and had two children. This marriage ended in divorce however, and Barbara took back her maiden name.

By 1984, Schaeffer had become an elder in

the Presbyterian Church. She participated in the international Witness for Peace service organization as a special education teacher and social worker, visiting Honduras and Nicaragua on a fact-finding mission involved with the Contra war.

"I found out first-hand about homeless people's needs from aiding refugees from Central America and Hispanic migrant workers."

Returning to Skagit County, Schaeffer met Barbara Cram at a meeting with women who had been involved with the development of homeless shelters. They continued to meet with others interested in this purpose, including a visit to California to see other shared housing sites.

"1985 went quickly, and by 1986 Friendship House was able to move into the house on Third Street with the help of my former husband."

Schaeffer continued to be involved with Friendship House after it opened, serving on the Board or pitching in with cooking or other chores. When Buzzy Marsh resigned in November 1998, Barbara Schaeffer was named as Director.

Schaeffer was very involved with activities for residents in the houses, as well as fundraising from many sources. She presented a number of reports to the Mount Vernon City Council that included requests for funds. She became concerned about the extremely limited options for affordable permanent housing for low-income residents and worked for some time on the idea of opening a third homeless shelter. Initially, the organization wanted to buy the old Salem Lutheran Parsonage just across the street from the shelters; however, it was sold before the group could make an offer.

Schaeffer describes a peculiar experience with the Board President in the fall of 2000. She had taken a week off to visit family in Eastern Washington. When she returned, she was informed that the Board President had called an unscheduled meeting that lacked a quorum. In her absence, it had been decided that Mary K James, former Women's House manager, had been hired as Director, and Schaeffer was to become director of Development and Fundraising.

Schaeffer still does not know how or why this was done, but she left Friendship House and became the Director of the Skagit County LOVE INC program.

Mary K. James (2000-2010)

Mary K. was born in Atlanta, Georgia in 1950. Her father was a Methodist minister, and he served in a variety of churches for many years, moving his family with him. She recalls moving to Indiana, and then to California with her sister and two brothers.

"I never spent more than 3 years in a school during my childhood," she states.

After graduating high school, Mary K. returned to Georgia and attended Reinhardt College for the next two years, earning an AA in Sociology. Memories of California called her and she moved back, getting training as a psychological technician. She was employed at Camarillo State Hospital for three years, enjoying the work but wanting more education.

Moving to Santa Barbara, Mary K. entered University of California Santa Barbara and completed a BA in Psychology. From 1972-1981 she received training in Community Psychology and worked in Santa Barbara Mental Health, participating in outpatient and inpatient services. She married Steve James and earned a MA in Public Administration.

Mary K and her family moved to Concrete, WA in the late nineties. Her husband began work in environmental services, while her daughter was attending college at University of Puget Sound in Tacoma. Living in Concrete, Mary K. began looking for work in Skagit County social services and was hired as Friendship House Women's House manager in 1997.

By 2000 she had been promoted to Friendship House Director. Mary K. worked to raise funds for many years, making a number of requests for help from the City of Mount Vernon and other sources. She was the longest serving Director, completing ten years in 2010. She retired to move to Eugene, Oregon to help care for her elderly mother who was living alone. Currently she works with Peace Health, a local hospital in Eugene, with the Heart and Vascular Services program. When her mother no longer is with her, she plans to retire and move to Australia where her daughter and grandchildren now live.

Marie Marchand (2011-2014)

Marie Marchand was born in Staten Island, New York and grew up in Denver, Colorado. After graduating from high school, she moved to Seattle and worked in the Kerner Scott

House, a mental health transitional housing setting, during 1989-1990. This experience was very influential, leading her to return to Colorado for university training. She earned a BA and MA in Social Justice Ministries. Moving west again, Marchand worked in Bellingham for the Whatcom Peace and Justice Center for more than five years.

For the first time in its history, Friendship House had advertised that it was seeking a new Director. Marchand applied and was hired.

"It suited my Social Justice background."

She received training from Mark Hanes, an interim director who was hired to develop the Board and hire a new Director.

Hanes was impressed by Friendship House, saying, "People are really generous to Friendship House--it's a transformative place!"

Marchand began working in 2011. She describes her first day:

"The day I walked into the men's house and saw the limited space of the community kitchen, I knew there had to be a new place for this service."

This concept became a primary focus of her work for the next three years. She fundraised in the community, participating with many people in many ways.

 One example of the connections she made was Fashions for Friendship, an event that was staged as New York-style fashion show complete with a runway, music, and lighting. This event featured 20 unique designs created with clothing originally found in Friendship House's clothing donation room and transformed into "fashion forward" outfits. Eleven designers repurposed garments. As each model walked the runway, a picture of the original clothing was shown on a screen. Five judges determined the winning designs of one adult outfit and one children's outfit based on creativity and presentation.

Marchand developed a partnership with the Fire Department working with Station 1 in Mount Vernon to spread the word about Friendship House as a cold weather shelter. Small emergency kits for were provided to firefighters to dispense which include blankets, something to eat and drink, hand-warmers, hats and information about meal times. The cold-weather shelter opens when temperatures hit freezing.

Marchand also completed Leadership Skagit, a nine-month program that includes cross-sector relationship building with a broad range of community residents. These may include judges, mayors, and technology managers; farmers and actors and persons with mental illness and children of the Swinomish Tribe. Marchand enjoyed working with others in the county and the positive connections which were made.

Marchand addressed the Mount Vernon City Council in March, 2012 concerning the serious discussion regarding public panhandling. She encouraged the Council to keep the dignity of vulnerable people and respect of public safety, civil liberty and common good in mind when developing any ordinance that would control or limit panhandling.

"The Friendship House is a resource center that does not promote panhandling, but is designed as a resource that plays a vital role in ending the cycle of homelessness by addressing the underlying and intersecting causes of homelessness....Panhandling deepens the social stigma of homelessness...there are a wealth of resources in Skagit County that makes panhandling unnecessary."

The community kitchen now known as Friendship House Cafe was a very major addition spearheaded by Marchand. Nearby property was purchased that included three deteriorated buildings that had to be removed. Fundraising was successfully accomplished with a number of grants and donations from local sources. A significant strength includes the program Hunger to Hope that includes basic cooking skills and kitchen support, as well as assistance with job search in the restaurant job market. The Cafe was opened December 23, 2013.

In 2014, Marchand moved on to a position in Bellingham, working as Legal Assistant to the City Council. However, she feels that eventually she would like to return to working for a non-profit.

"I like to help make a change in society."

Tina Tate (2014-Present)

Tina Tate was born and raised in Dallas, Texas. She was married at 15, and had her first son at age 16. Having dropped out of high school, she got her GED at 17. She moved with her husband and children to Pittsburg, Pennsylvania where they lived for two years and were divorced. She then moved to Corpus Christi, Texas where she married her second husband. He was in the Navy and took the family to Washington State, where they moved to Burlington. Here Tate had her second son and attended Skagit State College. A daughter was later born, but there were problems leading to a difficult breakup. Tate moved to California for a time, but the children were with her husband, so she returned to Skagit County where the divorce was finalized.

The return to the Skagit Valley marked a very difficult time in her life. She ended a relationship with a man she had been dating in 2000 and both of her parents died. She moved to Portland and began a period of serious drug and alcohol abuse. This was supported by work as a bartender but was a struggle just to get by.

"I hit rock bottom," Tate describes.

She became homeless and slept outside, grieving loss of contact with her beloved children who remained with her former husband in Skagit County.

"I struggled to save a bit of money and not use the drugs--by August 2004 I had just enough money for a bus ticket north."

Tate ended up in Mount Vernon, Washington and entered Friendship House holding a single bag of her belongings.

"It was such a relief!"

She stayed in Friendship House for six months, then moved into transitional housing. In October 2004, Skagit Publishing offered her a job telemarketing and answering phones. This position suited her very well, and she moved into full time customer service and later promoted to Supervisor and Circulation Manager. Tate was pleased to experience many trainings and learn a great deal during her ten years of employment.

The transitional housing setting was useful and stabilizing and eventually lead to sharing housing with friends elsewhere. As her career and income stabilized, Tate was able to purchase her own home, where she continues to live along with her daughter.

Tate was pleased to support Friendship House by becoming a member of the Board of Directors in June 2009. Tate's abilities were well recognized and she was elected Board President a little over a year later, in December 2010. By August 2014 she had been hired as Executive Director of Friendship House.

"I always wanted to make a difference, and take care of others," Tate says.

Tina Tate exemplifies the power of the Friendship House to support those whose lives have become overwhelmingly difficult, and who are willing to accept help to change. She has become involved with many aspects of community organizations in the county, and has implemented ongoing successful fundraising. Her personal history has given her powerful insight to the needs of others, and the heart to continue in a leadership role.

DONORS

Over the many years of Friendship House history, funding services has been a demanding issue. There have been periods of serious difficulty when requests for support from the community were raised and found warm giving response. At this time, community support is seen as a strength.

The Jack and Shirley McIntyre Foundation has been a lead donor in the community, pledging to fund half of the estimated cost of the Friendship House Cafe if the other half was matched by June 2013. This community match was included with the project's community introduction and received a generous response. The Cafe is now up and running well, of course! The McIntyre Foundation also came forward to pay off the mortgage on the transitional Oak House.

A long list of donors was presented in the August 2015 Friendship Times. These include the Faithful Friends Club's monthly donors. As these are current times, donations may be made via electronic funds transfer through a bank account or credit card. Fundraising now includes interesting local events such as the Skagit Fashion Week. A number of professional services are also supporters.

VOLUNTEERS

Judy Thorsland

Growing up in South Seattle, Judy was raised Catholic.

"I knew when I was young that the church values weren't correct."

She married young and had a son, then began using drugs. For ten years she used heroin, meth and alcohol, before getting into recovery. The experience gave her an awareness of the needs of users, and she began to work with others. She started a recovery center in Seattle called Genesis House, which involved methadone maintenance. This center was her practice in 1970-1973.

"The old systems of treatment were punishing," she said.

She relapsed and became homeless. Judy returned to Whidbey Island where she had lived previously. She had another son and connected with an evangelical church and with support got sober in 1982. From that point she was able to go back to community college where she earned an AA in 1986 and "found my identity."

While attending Skagit Community College in Mount Vernon, Judy began volunteering at Friendship House which had newly opened in 1986. She continued to volunteer to manage the House on weekends for three years. Simultaneously she attended Antioch College and earned a degree in Human Development.

With her degree Judy began working professionally in family support and then as intervention specialist until 2000. She became influenced by the work of Dorothy Day and the Catholic Worker Movement, and was called to Rochester, New York, the "Murder Capitol of New York." There she stayed for a year at a Catholic Worker house, serving meals to 50-100 people. Judy briefly returned to Whidbey Island, but felt called to return to New York. There she stayed until 2010, working to rehab three houses as the successful shelter community developed.

After finally returning to Langley on Whidbey Island, Judy became aware of the needs of homeless people on the Island. She began working with others as the chair of a coalition to develop a homeless House of Hospitality. There were no shelters for the homeless in the area, and statistics indicated that 400 people, 50% of whom were children, lacked permanent or stable housing. Fundraising succeeded in locating a House of Hope and securing a mortgage. The brochure given out by the Coalition cites Friendship House as a model for their vision:

"Friendship House's Transitional Housing Program is for residents who need extra time to gain stability and save money. The houses are run in an egalitarian manner, with additional oversight from the Transitional Housing Manager. Friendship House currently operates two houses in Mount Vernon."

Monthly Meal Club

Throughout Friendship House history, the kitchen has provided meals for many people in need of food. Even in the original house, the small old kitchen found volunteers from residents and the community to help provide ingredients and prepare meals.

Now that the Friendship House Cafe has been developed, volunteers still participate in serving meals. These helpful folk have been members of local churches and clubs primarily. A list of current Club providers may be seen in the Appendix.

RESIDENTS

Tim Hinds

Hinds grew up in Anacortes. He had a history of addictive behaviors, struggling with heroin, cocaine, marijuana and alcohol. He worked with the John King Recovery House in Mount Vernon for detox when he got to know Judy Thorslund. Judy was attending Skagit Valley College and volunteering at Friendship House and the Farmhouse residential home. Tim began to volunteer at the Farmhouse, a temporary community shelter, and moved into Friendship House in December 1988. After three months, he relapsed and had to leave the shelter, but he maintained a connection with Judy, who helped him get admitted to Isabella Recovery House in Spokane.

Hinds struggled with recovery, supported by keeping a journal and writing to Judy and others. After a few days he began to describe supporting others, getting positive feedback over time about how easy it was to talk with him. Hinds kept moving successfully through the system levels, but not without emotional struggle. He became a good peer leader, always observing himself and others.

He wrote in his journal, in April of 1989, "I'm beginning to take every day as it comes and I'm trying to enjoy and get the most out of every one. I don't want to waste my time feeling sorry for myself. I know there will be some days that I don't feel very good, but they're getting fewer...I've grown a lot. I'm not what I want to be, I'm not what I'm going to be, and thank God I'm not what I used to be."

Tim discharged after six months and moved back to Langley where he stayed outside Genesis House, a women's shelter managed by Judy Thorslund (Named after the one she had opened many years before in Seattle.) Sober, he worked as a handyman, then in tree service for three years. Eventually he took over Classic Construction, a business he is still running. He now owns 20 acres with five rental houses.

Barb Welsh

Barb grew up in Mount Vernon. She moved to Alaska as young adult, working as a bank teller in Anchorage and a cook for seven years. After returning to Skagit County, she married a fisherman who also made money dealing drugs. Welsh became an addict, and was in and out of treatment for a number of years. The couple had a daughter, who was supported with Barb by the grandmother. This caregiver passed away young and Barb lost custody of her daughter to her sister.

Barb drove to Yakima and stayed there alone for some time. Eventually feeling shameful, she returned to Mount Vernon. She was able to enter Friendship House when Buzzy Marsh was Director, staying for eight months. This began a major change in her life. Welsh recruited many helpers for the house, and began working at a refinery and attending church. The church bought her a car, and she continued to work at different jobs. While living in the women's house, she became friends with a resident living in the men's house. This was Carl, who joined with her in a move into shared housing. They were married for ten years, until he passed away.

Welsh got work at Job Corps as a cook, where she spent 15 years, becoming Senior Cook after three years. She learned to mentor kids--"they gave me back ten". Her health was troubled by Hepatitis C. "I learned a lot of lessons...I died several times, but came back in the hospital and eventually it went away." She has had four back surgeries and must take pain meds.

Now Barb lives in the Vintage Apartments in Mount Vernon, where she enjoys knowing everyone and always helps others. "My purpose is giving back." Welsh volunteered at Friendship House until her back pain got too bad, so her focus is on her apartment neighbors. Her energy is upbeat and positive. "I am close to my daughter now and love my two grandkids!"

AFTERWORD

Statewide Homelessness

Even though Washington State has one of the highest minimum wages in the country, it is still not enough to afford adequate market rate housing in many parts of the state. Seattle has been identified as the fastest growing city in the nation, with some of the largest companies in the world. Consider Amazon, Microsoft, Boeing, Starbucks...and yet, many families are being forced to choose between paying rent and putting food on the table.

King County has allowed tent cities for the homeless since 1990. Since 2008, 16 different properties in Seattle have hosted "Nickelsville" sites, named after Gregory Nickels, who was mayor at the time. A number of different churches have allowed homeless tents on their properties. There are a good variety of shelters that have been developed in King County and many places in the state. However, the Homeless Count for 2015 in Seattle was 3772 outside plus 6500 in shelters and transitional housing. Of the youth (13 to 18), half of all are runaways.

There are a number of services for veterans. The Veterans Assistance program offers Compensated Work Therapy, Supported Employment, and Supportive Housing (Section 8). However, there are frequent reports about veterans who are homeless with unaddressed needs such as Post Traumatic Stress Disorder. It can take time to connect with services.

The Bill and Melinda Gates Foundation includes a focus on homelessness in King, Pierce, and Snohomish Counties in Washington. Their program Building Changes has a Washington Youth and Families Fund: connecting the dots between Housing, Homelessness and Health Care. A major focus is finding and assisting with affordable housing for families.

The model that Friendship House has developed over the past 30 years includes elements that are fundamental for human needs. Yes, everyone needs a safe, warm place to sleep and food. In addition, there is the essential element of supportive community. If there is someone who can listen to you, give you time to feel safe and consider what the next step can be, connect with a longer term place to stay and safety for your children, find job possibilities and trust people around you, then your life will begin to change for the better. That is the meaning of homeless hospitality.

CONNECTIONS

Shelter

Men's Emergency Shelter

1008 S. Third St
360-336-2135

Women & Children's Emergency Shelter

922 S Third St
360-336-2418

Transitional Housing Program

Food

Friendship House Cafe
108 Snoqualmie St
360-873-8022

Weekday Meals:
7:00 am, 11:30 am, and 5:30 pm

Weekend Meals:
8:00 am, 12:30 pm, and 5:30 pm

Support

Hunger to Hope

Employment Training

No-cost Clothing and Essential Needs Bank

Open Tuesday and Thursday from 10 am to 3 pm

Case management, information & referrals

www.skagitfriendshiphouse.org

Business Office

922 S. Third St (rear building)
Mount Vernon, WA 98273
360-336-6138
360-336-5838 (fax)

Monthly Meal Club

Avon United Methodist Church

Bethany Covenant Church

Edison Lutheran Church

Fir-Conway Lutheran Church

First Christian Church

First Lutheran Church

Hillcrest Christian Fellowship

Mt. Vernon Kiwanis Noon Club

Mt. Vernon Presbyterian Church

Mt. Vernon SDA Church

North Cascades Christian Fellowship

Sacred Heart Church

Saint Paul's Episcopal Church

Salem Lutheran Church

Sonrise Christian Center

Saint Charles Church and

Immaculate Conception

ACKNOWLEDGMENTS

Beginning on the journey of pulling together information about this history required connecting with many different people.

Former Friendship House Board members included Buzzy Marsh, Cathie Wyman and Teddie Bordner.

Important founding partner and first Director Barbara Cram has passed, but Pat Simpson was able to provide a good deal of historic information and pictures. She also referred me to Judy Thorslund, who has currently demonstrated the impact of the Friendship House model in organizing a homeless shelter in Langley, WA.

My husband, Nick Pettit, and son Anthonio Miguel Bishop Pettit had useful recommendations about expanding the history to include national homelessness as well as current wider state responses. Anthonio has been a powerful editor and electronic organizer. David Slabaugh was the initial editor for written draft. Former residents Tim Hinds and Barb Welsh gave stories demonstrating the powerful life-changing experience of Friendship House.

Dennis Taylor, Tom Rose, and Don Summers were current and former Board members whose interviews provided helpful information.

All living directors, past and present, shared their personal life histories and experiences that are essential to the story: Buzzy Marsh, Barbara Schaeffer, Mary Kay James, Maria Marchand, and Tina Tate.

I am so grateful for all these wonderful people and send out thanks to all!

SOURCES

City of Mount Vernon, Washington

Ellsberg, Robert, ed. *Dorothy Day, Selected Writings: By Little and By Little.* New York: Orbis Books, 1992.

Hinds, Tim. Personal journal, 1989.

Hirsch, Kathleen. *Songs From the Alley.* New York: Ticknor & Fields, 1989

Marsh, Barbara. *Transitional Housing As Done at Friendship House 1990-2002.*

Nouwen, Henri. *Out of Solitude,* 1974. *Reaching Out,* 1975. Quoted in Friendship House discussion document.

Skagit County Community Action Agency

INDEX

Made in the USA
San Bernardino, CA
01 December 2016